Faithful
Meditations for Altar Guild

Caroline Conklin
Christopher L. Webber, Series Editor

MOREHOUSE PUBLISHING
Harrisburg, Pennsylvania, USA

Anglican Book Centre
Toronto, Canada

Copyright © 2000 by Caroline Conklin

Morehouse Publishing   **Anglican Book Centre**
P.O. Box 1321   600 Jarvis Street
Harrisburg, PA 17105   Toronto, Ontario, Canada M4Y2J6

Morehouse Publishing is a division of The Morehouse Group.

All rights reserved. No part of this book may be reproduced or transmitted in any form or by any means, electronic or mechanical, including photocopying, recording, or by any information storage and retrieval system, without written permission from the publisher.

First Edition   1   3   5   7   9   10   8   6   4   2

Unless otherwise noted, the Scripture quotations contained herein are from the New Revised Standard Version Bible, copyright © 1989 by the Division of Christian Education of the National Council of the Churches of Christ in the U.S.A. Used by permission. All rights reserved.

Library of Congress Cataloging-in-Publication Data

Conklin, Caroline.
   Meditations for altar guild members / Caroline Conklin.
      p. cm. — (Faithful servant series)
   ISBN 0-8192-1845-6 (pbk. : alk. paper)
   1. Altar guilds — Episcopal Church — Meditations.
   I. Title. II. Series.
   BX5948.C66 2000
   242'.69—dc21   00-021524

Passages marked BCP are from *The Book of Common Prayer* (U.S.A.). Passages marked BAS are from or are similar to the *Book of Alternative Services* (Canada). Hymn lyrics are from *The Hymnal 1982* © 1985 by the Church Pension Fund. Passages marked CP are from *Common Praise* (Canada), and passages marked 1938 are from the *Book of Common Praise* 1938 (Canada).

Printed in the United States of America

Cover design by Corey Kent

Contents

———— "You Were Chosen" ————

Were you chosen to read this book? Perhaps it was given to you in a public ceremony or maybe it was handed to you with a quiet "you might like to look at this." Maybe, on the other hand, it reached out to you in a bookstore and said, "Buy me!" Many books choose us in such ways and this book is likelier to have done so than most. But however this book came to you, it almost certainly happened because you have also been chosen for a ministry in the church or for church membership. Perhaps you hadn't considered this as being chosen; you thought you decided for yourself. But no, you were chosen. God acted first, and now you are where you are because God took that initiative.

God acts first—the Bible is very clear about that and God acts to choose us because God loves us. And who is this God who seeks us in so many ways, who calls us from our familiar and comfortable places and moves us into new parishes and new roles? Christians have been seeking answers to that question for a long time.

Part of that answer can be found within the church. We come to know God better by serving as church members and in church ministries. God is present with us and in others all around us as we worship and serve. But there is always more, and God never forces a way into our hearts. Rather, God waits for us to be quiet and open to a deeper relationship.

And that's what this book is about. This is not simply a book to read but to use, in the hope that you will set aside some time every day for prayer and the Bible—and for this book. So give yourself time not only to read but also to consider, to think about, to meditate on what you have read. The writers of these short meditations have been where you are, thought about their experiences deeply, and come to know God better. Our prayer is that through their words and experience and your reflection on them, you will continue to grow in knowledge and love—and faithful service—of this loving, seeking God.

— Christopher L. Webber
   Series Editor

Preface

When I became an Altar Guild member, the director explained that membership was a privilege. I heard what she was saying, but I wasn't convinced. The list of things we had to do seemed overwhelming—and definitely chore-like!

That was years ago, and gradually I have come to learn that she was right. We members are privileged, immensely so, and our tasks have great worth.

Our tasks have worth because we provide what the clergy and the community need in order to celebrate Holy Eucharist. But they have worth for other reasons as well: for the intrinsic value of the objects we handle; for the sacred space where they are housed; for the legacy of those who have performed these same duties over the years; for God's people who have come to this altar, and countless other altars, throughout the centuries; for God's people who will come in the future; for what we, working as partners, bring to our job and for what we take away from it.

The silver we shine, the wood we polish, the cloths we launder and iron, the wine and wafers we set out, the candles we replenish all serve to remind us that the active, willing hand of every Christian is needed to keep the Church alive.

Especially I have come to believe that we members of the Altar Guild are privileged because we experience regularly and uniquely the thinness of the veil between the sacred and the ordinary.

———— Serving the Servant ————

He came and took her by the hand and lifted her up. Then the
fever left her, and she began to serve them.

—*Mark 1:31*

Behind our altar is a reredos, a large wooden carving of the Last Supper designed after da Vinci's painting. It is nearly a century old, and precious. We are not to dust it; it's cleaned professionally. But we can gaze at it as much as we like! Jesus, in the center, wears such a sad, loving look that he always brings reflection and consolation.

The people at the table are carved against a flat wooden background. Behind that wood, I can almost see other people. I can almost catch glimpses of those who baked the bread, laid the cloth and dishes on the table, poured the wine, replenished the food, and afterwards washed up. The people I imagine are servants. Most of them, like most of us on Altar Guilds, are women.

Jesus in the carving isn't looking at the workers back there in the shadows, but that doesn't mean he has forgotten them. We know how he cherished and respected the women who talked with him, ministered to him, came to him for help. Unlike most men of his time, Jesus treated women as equally made in God's image. He also valued servanthood and thought of himself as a servant, too.

Sometimes as I prepare for the Eucharist at my church I imagine other women, those who served at the same altar from the last decade of the nineteenth century throughout the twentieth. They, like I, laid on the white cloths, arranged the vested chalice, tended to the candles, and set out the bread and wine. Like the servants at the Last Supper, they are gone from our sight but not from the sight of God. Their names may be lost from our memories, but they are never lost from the memory of God.

In most church art, the people portrayed tend to be male and famous, people named in the Bible or in Christian history. But we anonymous Faithful Servants ought not to let that bother us. With a light heart, knowing our worth in God's sight, we can let Jesus take us by the hand and lift us up. With a glad heart, fully aware of our value, we can serve the One who said he had come to serve.

᠁

A Set-Apart Space

God be in my head, and in my understanding;
God be in mine eyes, and in my looking;
God be in my mouth, and in my speaking;
God be in my heart, and in my thinking;
God be at mine end, and at my departing.

—*Hymnal, #694; 1938, #567*

I dash through the back door of the church from the parking lot. Late again! I toss off my coat. In the sacristy, my assigned partner smiles as she sets flowers in the brass vases that will stand on the retable behind the altar.

"Sorry!" I say. "My daughter called as I was leaving!"

I consult the checklist for this Saturday. "Okay, let's see. Did you dust? Yes? I'll polish the lectern."

I peer into the supply cupboard, grab the tin with the polishing material, and head across the hall toward the vast, high-ceilinged sanctuary. But before I can plunge through the door, something stops me short, something in the air that moves toward me from that sacred space.

I bow my head, draw a long breath, and pray for mindfulness. *God be in my head, eyes, mouth, heart...*

Then I step back across the hall to where my partner is examining a yellow blossom that seems less than fresh.

"How are you?" I ask her. "What's been happening in your life?"

She turns and tells me, and then I tell her. As we talk, we work through our checklist of chores. Eventually I sit on the red-carpeted steps leading to the chancel and polish the lectern. A few feet away sits my partner, polishing the pulpit.

Slowly, slowly the minutes unfold. There's no rush in here, no hurry. Outside, maybe, but not in here. Sometimes we laugh together, or we grieve together the recent loss of a friend. Sometimes we are companionably silent.

Time passes, of course, but not the way it does in other places. The very air of that set-apart space calms and soothes, as though the prayers and communion of countless worshiping parishioners have left behind an aura that recalls to us God's presence.

Soon, too soon, the checklist is completed. All is ready for Sunday worship. Warmly, we say goodbye. "See you soon! Take care!"

Before going back out to my car, I pray once more: *God be at my departing.*

I'm back in the everyday world now, but with a difference. My Altar Guild work has reminded me that all our tasks require care, mindfulness, and time. All our tasks, whether done alone or shared, are ultimately accomplished for one another and for God.

Wings

. . . and the angels waited on him.

—Mark 1:13b

One of our young rectors whose former parish was too small for an Altar Guild was used to doing everything himself. Naturally, he was grateful for our ministry. One day he exclaimed, "You ladies are angels sent from heaven!"

He moved away years ago, but we sometimes still laugh about that. The other day a seasoned member came to work and said, "My left upper back has ached for a week now. I must have slept wrong on one of my wings."

"Or," I said, "maybe God is tugging on that wing, trying to get you to go in a direction you haven't thought of yet!"

"Let's hope it hasn't been pulled completely off," a new member said. "A one-sided angel is a pitiful sight to see."

"Maybe," I said, "your wings are growing. Have you done something especially good lately?"

Someone else said, "I only wish one of you ladies with her wings still intact would fly up and wash that dirty ledge under the stained glass windows!"

Well, all right. It is pretty funny. But what do angels do? Angels wait on, angels watch out for, angels make things right. All of us understand these things. All of us do them.

My belief is that anyone can act as an angel to another person by performing whatever out-of-the-ordinary service is needed at the time. The young man who encouraged our son Matthew through Marine boot camp is an angel in my eyes. So is the friend who sat with me after our older son Tom died in a car accident, listening again and again to the same facts, the same wishes, the same regrets. So is the unknown woman who helped our stranded daughter find her way through the streets of Los Angeles when Sarah was temporarily partially sighted because of an eye disease. In my prayers I thank God for them and I wish them the best, all those countless people who have helped our family in large and small ways as we've moved blindly through our lives. In my prayers I ask God for the compassion and insight to help other human beings along their difficult, unseen paths.

Perhaps this very day will bring an opportunity for you or for me to accumulate a few more of those invisible, weightless, silky white feathers!

߷

Jesus Is Coming

Therefore you also must be ready, for the Son of Man is coming at an unexpected hour.

—*Matthew 24:44*

Jesus is coming for dinner! He'll be here in a few hours! There was a message on my voice mail when I got home today. He's bringing a few friends. I didn't catch all the names…Mary, Peter, Martha, James…and of course there are Bill and I. The message said eight or ten altogether. Luckily that's about what my table will hold, with the leaf in.

The message also said not to buy anything special. Good, because there's no time for that anyway. Let me think. I have some chicken in the freezer. You can do a lot with chicken. In the fridge we still have plenty of potatoes and carrots from the garden.

But what about the table service? What about the bread and wine? We have to have bread and wine!

I remind myself to calm down, to breathe deeply. I pray: *God above me. God beside me. God guiding my steps.*

That's better. Now.

Table service. We'll use our wedding china, white with a delicate wheat pattern, and our good silverware.

Bread. No time to bake, since I don't do it regularly and it takes me forever. Fortunately there's a loaf in the freezer from the batch I baked a couple of months ago.

Wine. Do we have any in the house right now? Yes! On my closet shelf is a bottle of red table wine we bought when my parents lived in the Napa Valley, before Father died and Mother moved here. I was saving it for a special occasion. Now I know what the occasion is!

The bread we can pass around and lay on our side plates. But the wine needs a special cup. I don't have a special cup! Still, with only ten of us, a stemmed wineglass should be large enough.

Why don't I have a white tablecloth? Didn't I, at one time? Well, the ivory one will have to serve. At least it's clean and not very creased.

All done. He'll be here any minute! Oh, but everything looks shabby, thrown-together, completely inadequate! I tried so hard but it isn't good enough, couldn't be...

He's coming, no matter what.

Would I rather he did not?

Oh no! No! I want him with us more than anything!

A quiet inner voice comforts me: *Then everything will be all right. You'll see.* Of course it will be! It always is.

As we prepare the table and the Eucharistic meal for Christ's weekly coming, let us remember that the meals he shared and the first meals in his name were in homes, not cathedrals, homes that were often poor in furnishings but always rich in devotion. Let us remember that Christ cares little for appearances and much for the welcoming heart.

Consider the Lilies

Give us all a reverence for the earth as your own creation, that we may use its resources rightly in the service of others and to your honor and glory.

—Book of Common Prayer, 388

These are the flowers I'm to set out on the retable behind the altar: two large pink roses; small pink and yellow lilies with strong purple stripes and delicate pink stamens, larger ones that are pink with flecks of purple; little purple carnations; white, yellow-centered daisies; dark green frothy ferns.

I place the flowers in their brass vases, where the congregation can consider them as they wait for the service.

We city dwellers spend much of our time indoors even in summer and don't get a chance to look at flowers as often as might be good for us. Some weeks or months, the only ones we see are behind the altar. How little space they take up, and yet how vitally important they are to the peace, the mood, the atmosphere of the church!

Some say that people are born with a built-in love of nature, with the knowledge that we are an integral part of the larger creation. I believe it. One of my earliest, shiniest memories is of walking hand in hand with my big sister down a suburban Cleveland sidewalk: passing first a white-fenced garden that was lavish with pink, red, blue, yellow, orange, white, and purple flowers—a garden buzzing with bees and marvelously fragrant—and continuing on past an empty lot filled with Queen Anne's lace, stopping to search out the jewel-like, deep purple treasure in each blossom.

Maybe there were two separate walks, and maybe the field and the garden weren't exactly as I recall. No matter. The wonder is that the memory has stayed with me all these years. Somehow my young human heart and soul must have required those flowers in order to grow.

Both Old and New Testament writers, and Jesus himself, use countless images from nature. I believe today's worshipers respond to them, even if we've only seen grapevines or fig trees or field lilies in pictures. Something deep within us knows what these things are and what they mean.

In our church we traditionally have no altar flowers during Lent, although I understand this isn't universally true. It certainly adds to our sorrow and our penitence not to see them there. Parishioners realize something's lacking, although they may not be too sure at first what it is. "Isn't the altar darker?" "Something's wrong this morning."

As we place the flowers near the altar, as we thank God for them, let us resolve to be less wasteful of our precious environment. Let us resolve to ensure that our children and grandchildren, and theirs, may wander through fields and gardens that will nourish their young hearts and souls.

৵

The Sparrow

Are not two sparrows sold for a penny? Yet not one of them will fall to the ground apart from your Father...So do not be afraid; you are of more value than many sparrows.

—Matthew 10:29,31

Once a sparrow got into the sanctuary through one of the narrow windows that we open on warm days. The tiny creature fluttered, swooped, and banged against the fifty-foot ceiling. As we worked on Saturday morning we called and beckoned, trying to bring its attention to the still-open windows. Of course the sparrow didn't respond to us, and of course we laughed at ourselves for trying.

But we stopped laughing on Sunday. When I brought out the vested chalice, I nearly stepped on the bird's body behind the altar! Probably it had died of thirst or starvation. I carried it out and dropped it into the Dumpster with a word of gratitude for its brief life. I wished I could have given it a bit of a wafer, a sip of water when I had the chance. I wished I had tried harder to save it. Shouldn't I have called the Humane Society? Opened more windows, opened the doors? Persisted in urging it out to safety? That sparrow's death seemed somehow to be my responsibility.

I took comfort from knowing that God watched that sparrow's fall, that God the Creator of the world and all its beings knows and cares about what happens to each one of us and that nothing can happen in the universe without God knowing about it.

Later that morning, as I worshiped, it came to me that people in a church can sometimes flutter as helplessly and as hopelessly as that sparrow. People who are physically able to receive the bread and the wine may be sunk too far into despair, pain, or grief to receive any real nourishment from them. I've been there a few times myself, so I know. Yes, God watches them, but God charges me to do the same! The people in the sanctuary are my worshiping community, my parish family. If the little bird that wandered in by mistake was my responsibility, how much more so are the brothers and sisters who come in on purpose?

Next time we do our practical work at the altar, let us think of the people we know who are hurting and of practical ways we might help them. Let us pray for the insight to recognize signs of distress in people we don't know, so that we may not fail any one of God's precious beings who needs our help.

ॐ

Sailing in Troubled Seas

A windstorm swept down on the lake, and the boat was filling with water, and they were in danger. They went to him and woke him up, shouting, "Master, Master, we are perishing!" And he woke up and rebuked the wind and the raging waves; they ceased, and there was a calm.

—*Luke 8:23b–24*

Our church building is more than a hundred years old and made of solid, impenetrable stone. It's not like a biblical boat on a stormy sea, not at all. But as we read about church burnings and bombings, about hurricanes and tornadoes, we must realize that no building is indestructible. Anything humans have created, humans or nature can destroy.

A few years ago, Bill and I took a cruise through the Greek Islands. At Santorini, a lovely place with cliff tops made snowy by whitewashed houses, the harbor was too shallow for our ship to dock. We had to anchor off shore and take tenders, motorized lifeboats, the rest of the way.

The sea was rough over to the island. Our little boat was tossed high, side to side, bow to stern, and most of us got wet. But the ride back was worse. Abruptly, the tender stopped. Not only that, in the distance our mother ship began moving away from us. Our beautiful white ship, with all our belongings, with its kitchens and dining rooms and pools and lounges, was going, leaving us behind!

Because of the engine sounds of the little boat, the danger of moving around, and the language barrier between us and the Filipino crew, we couldn't find out what was happening. We could only wait, growing more and more uneasy.

What was wrong? Had we been forgotten? Was the ship hijacked or undergoing a bomb search? Sinking? People got quiet. Some of us bowed our heads, calling on God to attend us now that the going was rough.

Soon the cruise ship stopped and we began moving toward it again. Back on board, we were told that the ship's anchor had been dragging. The captain moved to locate a less sandy area of sea bottom so that the tender could return safely.

Like that tender, like that ship, like the boat in the Gospel, our beautiful church building is vulnerable. All the things we members tend, all our linens, vessels, vestments, furnishings, and art, could disappear forever. Would that destroy the parish church? It would not! People would open their homes for worship, would donate the objects and money needed. Eventually another building would be found or built. It might look quite different. No matter. God is present wherever two or three people gather to recall that God is there.

As we do our work for the church, even when our seas are smooth, let us wake to God. Let us remember the fragility of things and thank God for our strong community gathered.

৵

Mystery Doors

Ask, and it shall be given unto you, seek, and ye shall find, knock, and the door shall be opened unto you; Allelu, alleluia!
—*Hymnal, #711; CP, #458*

Our church is old, with a basement that is poorly lighted and maze-like. One locked door down there has an opaque colored-glass window and opens to a room filled with Altar Guild supplies that are used only occasionally. New members are taken to this room and shown the hidden key.

Until I was a member, I wondered about that door. Now when I locate the key and open it, I think back to a time when I was five and lived in Ohio. We had a large, tree-filled yard. On one of the trees was an oval area where the bark was gone and the bare trunk exposed. An older neighbor girl said, "That part is a magic door. Close by here there's a key-leaf. If you find the key-leaf and rub that part with it, the door will open and you'll see the stairs to fairyland!"

A little fearfully, in case it should be true, I tried every leaf in my yard and some from hers. She saw me and laughed at me for believing her. Ashamed, I stopped trying. In a way, I was relieved. If I had opened that magic door, what would I do? Leave my family, just like that? Still the idea was thrilling...think of it...to climb into a beautiful, wondrous new place...

Mystery doors, I believe, recall to us that no matter how many doors we've opened so far in our lives, there are many more to come. Always there will be unknown thresholds for us to cross until at last we reach the threshold to our heart's true home. We don't call it fairyland, though. We call it heaven.

Of course no locked door in any church, nor tree in any yard, will lead us there. But doors symbolize the Mystery. *Knock, and the door shall be opened unto you.* Yes! Perhaps we need the door as much as we need the promise that we will one day pass through it. We need the reminder that we have more to learn, farther to go, higher to grow, both in this life and in the next.

I hope that I may never be so sophisticated or so cynical that I stop yearning and searching for the key to God's ultimate Mystery.

ᢒ

The Healing Light of Advent

O God, you have caused this holy night to shine with the brightness of the true Light: Grant that we, who have known the mystery of that Light on earth, may also enjoy him perfectly in heaven.
—Book of Common Prayer, Christmas, 212;
Book of Alternative Services (Canada), 273

Four weeks ago, we hauled out the heavy iron Advent Wreath stand and filled the five candles with oil. Soon the white candle in the center will be lit, as a perfect fulfillment of the one pink and three purple candles that surround it.

Many of us have experienced at least one Christmas that was more sad than joyful, usually after a family member or close friend with whom we used to celebrate is no longer with us.

Our worst holiday season was after our three-year-old son Tom died in a car accident. I had a home Advent wreath for the first time that year, and I lighted the appropriate candles every Sunday.

But those candles have a distinctive fragrance, and memories evoked by smell are especially strong and deep-seated. For many years after that terrible year, I was unable to have a wreath in my house because the scent overwhelmed me with sorrow. Still, the wreath at the church kept the light alive in my heart even as the people of the parish, with their own stories of loss, helped me to remember that our family had not been singled out for grief.

Some years ago, a little girl from Sunday school handed me a bark-covered piece of wood with hollowed-out spaces for five thin, leaning candles. A few pieces of holly were crookedly pasted on. "For your house," she said, so what could I do but take it home? I did, and lit it, and was made glad!

Now when I help decorate the church with the poinsettia, the special candelabra, the star and the lights—as well as with the Advent candles—I send up a special prayer for those whose grief on this holy night is new, fresh, and raw. I ask that someone in our parish family be permitted to touch them in their sorrow as that little girl touched me.

I ask that they too may know the special healing mystery of the Light.

ॐ

First Be Reconciled

So when you are offering your gift at the altar, if you remember that your brother or sister has something against you, leave your gift there before the altar and go; first be reconciled to your brother or sister, and then come and offer your gift.

—Matthew 5:23-24

I don't believe it! The one member whom I find difficult is partnered with me this morning! How could the director make such a mistake? I've told her my preference as plainly as I can.

This person finds fault with my work. She finds fault with the rector, the vestry, the diocese, and the national Church. When she runs out of those complaints, there's always the weather. Her sour moods lower mine for the rest of the weekend.

Dear God, I pray, *help me to make it through the next hour calmly and with good grace.* I grit my teeth. "Nice morning."

"If you don't mind gale-force winds," she growls, her face looking even more disapproving than usual. She inspects my ironed linens. Two don't pass muster.

I smile, though I'm seething inside. "Oh dear! I'd better take these back home and try again."

I look at the checklist. Aren't there a few tasks we could skip this Saturday? Anything to get out of here fast!

She steps close, looking too. I can't help saying, "I didn't know you were on duty today."

"I asked to be changed."

"Ah." But I wish the director had warned me.

She goes on. "I can't work next week because my nephew in Omaha is having an operation, and I need to be there."

"Oh?" I say, turning to her. "Is it serious?"

To my dismay, I see her hard face begin to crumple. "They say he has only a fifty-fifty chance of surviving. He just turned twelve."

I touch her arm. Awkwardly, she sobs twice against my shoulder. I hold her and reach for a tissue, murmuring words that I hope will comfort. When she recovers herself, she's the same old gruff, critical person. Or is she? Her face and her words seem somehow softer now—unless it's my perception that has changed.

As we work together, carefully preparing for tomorrow's Eucharist, I plan to call the director and tell her it's okay if we're partnered again. Before we leave, I offer another hug. Shyly she accepts it.

Driving home, I cherish the reminder I've had that day. Only a heart free to give to a sister or brother can give freely to God in God's house.

༄

—— Smooth It Away ——

Every valley shall be lifted up, and every mountain and hill be made low; the uneven ground shall become level, and the rough places a plain.

—Isaiah 40:4

When the Eucharist is over, the Altar Guild members on duty in our parish take home the soiled linen corporals, lavabo towels, credence table cloths and purificators, as well as the various cloths used for cleaning and covering. We wash them in our own machines. The altar cloths we iron.

I understand that in many parishes the smaller wet linens are spread out on Formica and smoothed rather than ironed because the wear and tear on the fabric is less. But the principle is the same: eliminating those creases.

I never cared much for ironing. Possibly that's because I had to iron my father's white shirts for a period of a few weeks when I was a young teen. My mother got sick, a rare occurrence for her even now, and was hospitalized. I'm sure the shirts I ironed were awful. I'm sure Father had to wear his jacket all day, even in the pre-air-conditioned Washington, D.C., heat to hide the wrinkles. He didn't complain, exactly. But I knew.

My daughter and I have a running joke about my aversion to the job. "Sarah, what's that triangular thing with the handle and the cord that I see in your closet?"

"Never mind, Mom. You don't want to know."

But Altar Guild ironing is different. Altar Guild ironing I actually enjoy. As I push the heavy, hot implement over the steaming cloths, I do it in quiet. At the same time, prayerfully, I smooth out some of the wrinkles in my own life:

An obsessive worry over my son. Can I do anything about it at the moment? No. Smooth it away; give it to God. A put-down remark an acquaintance made yesterday. Is there something about myself I should change because of it? No, that particular problem is his. Smooth it away, give it to God. Harsh words spoken to a friend. There's something I can fix! Today I'll write her a note to say I'm sorry. Smooth it away; give it to God.

Afterwards I smile as I look at the pile of gleaming white cloths on my stair ledge, ready to be returned to the sacristy. I feel privileged that I have been allowed to carry visible symbols of God's grace into my home.

You and I may not need to iron anything at all today, or for many days. Meanwhile, let us remember that God will make level what is creased and uneven in all our lives, if only we take some quiet time to ask.

౨౿

The Christmas Creche

There was also a prophet; Anna...She never left the temple but worshiped there with fasting and prayer night and day. At that moment she came, and began to praise God and to speak about the child to all who were looking for the redemption of Jerusalem.
—Luke 2:36–38

We members may feel like Anna sometimes, especially at Christmas when the Guild is often shorthanded because of vacations. We may feel that we never leave the temple!

But in yet another way we are like Anna. Anna saw the baby Jesus, may have touched him, certainly recognized him for who he was. We also see, touch, and recognize the baby Jesus. Not in the flesh, of course. That happened once in history. But every year, most churches set up at least one nativity scene. In ours, we bring out lovely resin figures and set them in a child-sized wooden stable by the chancel steps. The baby we hold especially carefully. Why? Because it is fragile, because it represents Jesus, God made flesh.

Anna used her temple time well. She absorbed some of the past-present-future atmosphere that holy places have. How do we know that? Because she was a prophet, so wise that she could help people deal with what was happening today in the light of what had been and of what was to come. When she saw the baby, she realized something new was going on. Times were changing. For the better? Oh, yes! But only if the community cherished the child. No wonder she spoke to everyone who came by. They had to know about this! Now!

In our church we sometimes stage a Christmas pageant with a doll for the baby and children in all the other roles. In many such pageants adults perform too, but not in ours. The unfortunate side of our practice is that it tends to sentimentalize a story that is ultimately about tremendous risk and sacrifice. The happy side is that we affirm our belief in every child as worthy and capable of conveying our faith story.

And what a story it is! Two thousand years ago God chose to become vulnerable, helpless, dependent on human hands and hearts. Think of it!

As we gratefully prepare the sanctuary for Christ's Mass, may we, like Anna, forever cherish the child.

Having a Dress

[Jesus] said to his disciples, "Therefore I tell you, do not worry about your life, what you will eat, or about your body, what you will wear. For life is more than food and the body more than clothing."
— *Luke 12:22–23*

A legendary Boston lady was invited by her friends to go dress shopping. She raised her eyebrows in genteel surprise and said, "But I already have a dress."

She certainly didn't worry about what she would wear on any given occasion. Neither, as a rule, do clergy. From the Vesting Room closet they pick out something in basic white and the correct stole to go with it. There's ease in that for them, and release to focus on more essential things. Garments used by clergy in the service are traditional and simple because too much change or elaboration could distract us from the worship of God.

In our parish, with only one or two regularly serving clergy, the Altar Guild plays a minor role in the care of vestments. Still, we are aware of each item's name and purpose, and we take notice of those in obvious need of cleaning, pressing, or repair. We understand the importance of vestments in the setting that we have been charged to prepare for the Eucharist.

As we look with satisfaction at an orderly, uncluttered Vesting Room closet, let's think about our own closet, at home. Is it so full that we spend too much time fretting over what to wear? Do we try to make our clothes and not our selves express to the world who we are? Might simplification actually enrich our lives?

Mother's closet at the retirement home was piled and layered with clothing she never wore. She always put on the same two or three outfits, the ones on top of the stacks. My sister and I went in one day, pulled everything out, held up each item and asked Mother, "Keep or give to Goodwill?" ("Throw it out" is not in Mother's vocabulary.) Everything she rejected because of its uncomfortable fit or unbecoming style we took away. Since then she's been able to see each wearable item, and her functional wardrobe has actually expanded.

Of course it's easier to look at the Vesting Room closet, or someone else's, with detachment. But occasionally let's try to see our own as we see the others: objectively. Let's ask ourselves honestly what we need, what we like and what fits, and dispose of everything else. We may find ourselves with fewer garments but additional time to consider how much more than clothing there is to life—and to our God-imaged selves.

꒰꒱

Christ's Own

N., you are sealed by the Holy Spirit in Baptism and marked as Christ's own for ever. Amen.

—Book of Common Prayer, 308;
Book of Alternative Services (Canada), 160

Marked as Christ's own! Forever! Even copying these words down, I'm nearly moved to tears. I'd definitely cry if it weren't for that impersonal "N."

What a marvelous, wonderful, heavenly thing! To be marked as Christ's for eternity!

Of all the special settings we members prepare, the baptism setting is the hands-down favorite. In our church, we make ready a copper lining for the cement font, a heavy pewter pitcher for the warm water, a thin silver shell for pouring, a towel for the initiate's forehead, a screw-top oil stock, matches, a small baptismal candle for the family, and the tall Paschal candle. Then we move into the congregation and eagerly wait for the two-millennia-old, forever-new drama that will soon be enacted once more.

I remember my own baptism because my parents, even though they were churchgoers, postponed it until we were about to undertake a perilous car trip across the western United States for a book my father was writing on mine taxation. The trip was treacherous then in ways different from now, when high speeds and heavy traffic are our major concerns. Then highway systems were poor, service stations were few and far between, and cars tended to break down. I recall a whole series of flat tires, dripping oil pans, and overheated engines.

My parents believed that God would accept me into heaven, baptized or not, were I to die on the trip. But baptism was something they had intended to do someday, and before a long trip seemed as good a time as any. So at the age of six I was taken to church. I remember standing up alone and being spoken over by a kindly man, then bending my head to receive the water. I remember feeling important.

Much more clear in my mind are the baptisms of our four children, the two who were born to us and the two we adopted. Yet in a way I remember all the baptisms I've ever witnessed. And why not? Each is a welcoming into the household of God. Each little one, and older one, who comes to the font is part of our family. Every big-eyed, wobbly-necked infant; every solemn, nervous ten-year-old; every determined, devout adult—they are all my children, all our children. We may forget that sometimes, being human. Every baptism we witness reminds us.

William, Caroline, Sarah, Thomas, Mary, Matthew, Josh, Ashley, Rachel, Edward, you are sealed! You are marked! Forever!

May we never lose the miracle of it. May the tears of joy and wonderment never cease filling our eyes.

᠅

A Tiny Flame

Your eye is the lamp of your body. If your eye is healthy, your whole body is full of light; but if it is not healthy, your body is full of darkness.

—*Luke 11:34*

The sacristy candle by the aumbry that holds the reserve sacrament is housed in red glass within a brass enclosure and is suspended by a chain. It hangs well over my head. Changing the candle requires standing on a chair, pulling the red glass straight up inside the brass, then dealing with a second container that's hot and holds liquid wax. One person can do it, but it's a lot easier with two.

Approximately every fourteen days, the candle needs to be replaced. Exactly when to change it is a judgment call. Sometimes the flame is present, but too low to be seen from directly beneath.

My faith can be like that candle. Sometimes it's high and bright. But sometimes it's low and dim, nearly invisible.

One recent Saturday morning my faith was very low indeed. I'd prayed for direction but still wasn't sure of the best use of my time. I'd prayed for my daughter's peace of mind, but she was still in distress. I'd asked for safe travel for my friend, but an accident happened anyway. Going about my Altar Guild work, I complained to God. *Why?* I prayed. *Why do you seem so far from me, when I labor so faithfully in your vineyards, when I stand right here at your altar?*

But I held back my resentment and doggedly followed the checklist. Speaking in monosyllables to my partner, ignoring the worried look on her face, I removed fingerprints from the altar rail and vested the chalice. Back and forth from the sacristy to the chancel I trudged, bringing in what was needed for the Sunday services.

Then my partner called from the nave, "I was afraid the sacristy candle was completely out, but it isn't! It should last at least through the first service. There's still a tiny flame!"

A tiny flame? I stepped down to the nave and stood beside her, close beside her. Yes! There was a tiny flame! A tiny flame is all that's needed to indicate the presence of the sacred. A tiny flame by the aumbry. A tiny flame in our hearts.

I smiled at her, for the first time that morning. Looking relieved, she smiled back, laid her arm on my shoulders, asked me what was the matter. Finally I told her. Finally I recognized the help God had sent me in the first place! As she listened and sympathized, my burden of troubles seemed lighter, no longer impossible to bear.

May we always remember that it's easier with two.

꒰ꕤ

One Servanthood

Almighty and everliving God, ruler of all things in heaven and earth, hear our prayers for this parish family...Grant us all things necessary for our common life, and bring us all to be of one heart and mind within your holy Church; through Jesus Christ our Lord.
—Book of Common Prayer, 817

This happened years ago. The interviewing priest had asked about salary, housing, service times. "Is there anything else?" the search committee chair wondered.

He hesitated, and I think I almost saw sweat beads on his pale forehead. "What," he asked in hushed tones, "is your Altar Guild like?"

I was tempted to lean forward, widen my eyes and whisper, "Don't ask. Someday we'll tell you what happened to the last two rectors!"

I restrained myself. Keeping up the myth of Altar Guild members as dragon ladies was kind of fun. But it wasn't worth the harm it has caused us overall, just as any myth about a group of people causes harm to the individuals within it.

Where did the myth come from, anyway? While I don't really know, I suspect that when women's only role at the altar was to be on the Guild, and usually to be behind-the-scenes-invisible, we tended to a fussy sort of perfectionism. We may even have roared a little and breathed a little fire!

Times changed. Gradually girls became acolytes and women became readers. Then about thirty years ago, when women began to be ordained, every door of church service was thrown open to every person. We members were no longer the only women serving around the altar. Nowadays the acolyte, priest, lay Eucharistic minister, deacon, usher, reader, or visiting bishop is just as likely to be female as male. By the same token, in many parishes, men choose to be on Altar Guilds and families work together taking turns to dress the altar, just as in the old days when the Eucharist was held in homes.

As a result, we seasoned members have had to give up some of our scariness. That's okay! We can always wear a dragon mask when we open our doors to children on Halloween. The rest of the time, let's happily leave that mask on the shelf. Let us thank God for the healthy, healing change that makes each area of our common life in servanthood available to all.

Holy Stitchery

And the Lord God made garments of skins for the man and for his wife, and clothed them.

—*Genesis 3:21*

A few dedicated, talented people in our parish stitch altar linens. In the past, some have crafted needlepoint kneeling cushions, one with a unicorn on it, one with a Christ symbol, one with the Episcopal seal.

Church stitchery is a beautiful calling, and a holy one. We read that God was the first to fashion clothing. Probably Eve took inspiration from God's handiwork when she sat down to make garments for her little family.

Why Eve and not Adam? Because Adam was out in the field plowing and planting while Eve stayed close to home to bear, nurse, and raise the children. That is why women in every society have been the ones most often designated to sew, although many men have been called to the craft as well.

While I haven't tried church stitchery, I have done crewelwork, needlepoint and cross stitch for family projects. The slowed-down rhythm of it is almost like meditating.

Last month I worked on a Christmas stocking for twenty-month-old

Logan. When I showed it to him, he smiled and touched it with a small finger. "Baby," he said, and why he called it that only he will ever know. He didn't care that it wasn't perfect. He'll care even less when it's finished and filled with toys.

I expect young Cain and Abel smiled at Eve's stitchery like that.

But when I took the stocking back and looked at it, each mistake jumped out at me. Despite years of practice, I don't seem to progress much. I still miscount. I still sometimes work unevenly. The back of my work is jagged and crisscrossed with thread ends and long pieces stretched between color areas.

Might I do stitchery for the church? Holy stitchery? Oh, I don't think so! My family and friends have to tolerate my mediocre work. The church family does not.

But yesterday, when I began to sew again on the stocking, I could hardly see what I thought was so wrong before. It occurred to me that ever since Eve my stitching sisters and brothers have made mistakes too. Back at the church, I looked more closely at a pillow under an acolyte bench. Sure enough, there was a stitch or two out of place! Overall, it didn't matter a bit. The intended pattern and purpose came through.

I remembered then that God requires perfection only in our devotion to God, to our true selves, and to one another. My needlework, lovingly done, might be acceptable to the church family and to God after all. And so might yours. Shall we give it a try?

Sunday Best

How could we sing the LORD's song in a foreign land?
—*Psalm 137:4*

When we prepare the church for Sunday services, we are doing more than a series of chores. We are helping create a space and a time for God's people to be quiet, to rest, to restore their souls. More than that, we are moving ourselves and our congregations toward keeping one of the Ten Commandments. Nowhere else in our over-busy society is Sunday different, is Sunday best.

On Christmas or Easter afternoon I'm glad when I have an errand to run because I love to see the shopping malls empty and the streets nearly deserted. They used to be that way every Sunday. Years ago, most commercial activity stopped once a week. Money couldn't be made or retrieved or spent on the Sabbath. Only a few places stayed open for emergency food or medicine. It was a time for worship, and a time for family.

My own Sunday-after-church memories are sweet. Father lay on the sofa listening to a slow-paced baseball game. Mother sat nearby, leafing through a magazine while the pot roast simmered. My sisters and I, warmed by a cat or two, played on the rug with paper dolls. We were happily quiet together, and soon we would happily share Sunday dinner and conversation.

Of course Sundays in America have sometimes been oppressive. As a boy at the beginning of the twentieth century, my father had to wear tight scratchy clothing through long church services. The remainder of the day back home seemed even longer, because he and his brother were forbidden to laugh, play, or even read anything but the most edifying books. To him, Sunday-best meant boredom and discomfort.

Maybe the "blue laws" regulating Sunday commerce were gradually set aside by people who, like my father, shuddered at the memory of the Sundays of their youth.

But moving from severity shouldn't have to mean constant clamor and clatter with no distinction at all among the days. People aren't made for that. It tires us out. It wears us down. It wreaks havoc on our hearts, minds, and spirits. It isn't what God wanted for us, not at all.

As Altar Guild members, let us stay mindful of, and thankful for, the great service we do when we help set apart a sacred atmosphere at church. It is our privilege. It is our duty.

It is mandated by our God.

༜

The Rainbow

Look at the rainbow, and praise him who made it.

—Sirach 43:11

One of an Altar Guild's tasks is to make sure that use of color in the sanctuary is effective yet restrained, that the color there leads us toward celebrating God's glory rather than distracting us from it.

Vestments, frontals, veils, and burses are usually done in some combination of the seasonal colors. That may seem to be a restrictive palette, but wonderful things can be done with red, purple, black, white, green, blue, gold, and silver. Even the darkest, dimmest sanctuary can be brightened with flashes of color here and there. Color has the power to delight the human heart and lift the spirits as nothing else can. Look at the way sunsets delight us, and sunrises. Look at the rainbow.

Recently I was in Seattle in late spring, after an especially wet fall and winter. Suddenly someone in the house cried, "Come see! A rainbow! Hurry!" We all dashed out to the porch and stood there, gazing and exclaiming, until it was gone.

God gifted us with rainbows. We can bring a reminder of that gift not only to sanctuaries but to other places as well. Once I was in a hospital visiting a sick parishioner when another visitor brought her a coloring book and crayons. The sick woman was delighted, and then and there selected crayons for decorating the dress of a princess at a ball.

Remembering her delight, the next time I felt sad and downhearted I tried coloring-book therapy for myself. I found that the round wax stick fit like a memory between my fingers as the familiar fragrance rose to my nostrils. Under my moving hand, color gradually appeared in the fairy tale landscape where no color had existed before. It was something like the way color becomes rich and deep at sunset, eases into the world at sunrise, sweeps across the sky after a rain. Not much like those things, but something like. Enough like to remind us of the joy and hope of God's promise.

As we mindfully add color to our worship place, let us be glad of the power it has to please and encourage the human heart. Then, for the rainbow in the sky, the rainbow on the page, and the rainbow in the sanctuary, let us praise God!

Spilled Wine

And no one puts new wine into old wineskins; otherwise, the wine will burst the skins, and the wine is lost.

—Mark 2:22a

The new member was in tears.

"The funnel slipped as I was pouring wine into the cruet! Now look. There's wine all over the purificator and the corporal. I knew I couldn't do this job. I'm too awkward and careless!"

A seasoned member, one of those irritating people who always does everything exactly right without apparent effort, took the wet red cloths and carried them to the sink. Over the sound of the running water she said, "Reminds me of the time I dumped a whole cruet of wine over the fair linen, not fifteen minutes before the service was to start."

The new member and I stood transfixed. "Wow," I said. "When was that?"

"Oh, many years ago. Before you came."

"I'd have died!" the new member said, her voice trembling. "How did it happen?"

"I'm not sure. I was in a hurry because the congregation had begun to gather. Apparently my sleeve caught on something. Next thing I knew, there was the cruet, lying on its side. The corporal was soaked, also the fair linen and the pad underneath it, I shrieked, I think. If I didn't, I certainly felt like it."

"What did you do then?" the new member whispered.

"Well, the director came charging up out of the nave, beckoning a couple of other Altar Guild members along with her. Next thing I knew, the four of us were whipping things off, mopping things up, soaking things. We had another fair linen handy, so by service time everything looked pretty good. Later we had to work hard to get things really clean again. Not like now. This clean-up is a cinch."

She turned off the faucet. "There, you see? The stain hardly shows. I'll take these home and make them good as new."

The new member smiled. "Thank you so much! I'll try to be more careful from now on."

"I know you will. But if it happens again, no real harm done. God smiles, I'm sure."

Later, after the new member had gone happily home, I said to the seasoned member, "You never told me that story."

"Didn't I? Slipped my mind, I suppose. Hardly a time I'd want to remember."

But she wasn't meeting my eye, and something in her tone...

"It never happened!" I exclaimed.

She frowned. "No? Well, possibly not. Possibly I dreamed it. Anyway," she said firmly, "it certainly could have happened! To any of us."

Old wineskins are too hard and dry to accommodate the expansion of new wine. Have our self-concepts dried and hardened over the years? Or have we, like that seasoned member, the grace to give a little, the grace to relinquish some of our reputation for competence, in order to ease another's distress?

Sacred Oatmeal

O Food to pilgrims given, O Bread of life from heaven, O Manna from on high!

—Hymnal, #308, #309

We set out bread and wine on the credence table for a Eucharistic meal. It is different from all other meals, yet the same. Every food taken with our fellow pilgrims, whether family, friend, or stranger, is potentially meaningful. Partly because of our experience at the Eucharist, we understand how significant any meal can be if we make it so.

I don't like oatmeal, but I ate it once and relished it. I'll always be glad I did.

Some years ago my Aunt Dorothy, who was in her eighties, became mortally ill with ovarian cancer. Her daughter, my cousin Kathleen, took Dorothy into her home with hospice help. Toward the end, Kathleen invited me to Boise for a visit.

One June morning the three of us sat around the sunny kitchen table. My aunt was eating little by then. To tempt her appetite, Kathleen cooked oatmeal, Dorothy's favorite breakfast dish. "Do you want some?" she asked me.

"No, thank you," I said, automatically.

But then, by the grace of God, I realized that the breakfast wasn't about me, or about oatmeal. It was about being together in love. "I've changed my mind," I said. "May I have some, please?"

That shared oatmeal, with plenty of sugar and milk, tasted wonderful! The three of us dipped our spoons into the fragrant, steaming bowls. Aunt Dorothy, whose dry wit was unimpaired, discussed items from the paper and talked of days back on the Idaho farm with her five brothers and two sisters. She ate as much as she could of the oatmeal and then returned to her bed.

That was the last food Dorothy was to take at table. Two days later her pilgrimage ended, and she went home to God.

I still don't eat oatmeal, but I'll always be grateful for that special bowl and for the lesson I learned that morning: At the Communion table or away from it, shared meals may nourish more than the body.

When we eat a shared meal today, let us treasure the precious time that we have together on this earth even as we look forward to the life beyond this one, when we will gather once again for a feast at God's table.

～

─────── Straining at the Leash ───────

Dear People of God: The first Christians observed with great devotion the days of our Lord's passion and resurrection, and it became the custom of the Church to prepare for them by a season of penitence and fasting.

—Book of Common Prayer, Ash Wednesday, 264–265;
Book of Alternative Services (Canada), 281

For Ash Wednesday we switch to purple veil and burse, then set out ashes in a small container along with a rag and water for washing clergy thumbs.

As we work around the altar, we may personally prepare ourselves for the long Lent ahead by deciding what we're going to stop doing this year.

Sometimes giving up something can be freeing.

I've tried to explain this to my little terrier-mix Clare, named for the Saint Clare who founded a religious order.

Like a religious, Clare is poor and chaste. Is she obedient? It depends on your definition. She jumps on guests, demanding to be petted, and sits where she chooses. Sometimes people who meet Clare will comment casually on dogs they know who have benefited greatly from obedience school. I don't know why they do this. I'm happy with the way Clare is now. Usually. She's happy with the way she is, certainly.

Every morning she dogs my footsteps until I'm ready to take her for a walk, then leaps and spins for joy when I go for the leash. But then she bites and strains at her leash for about the first half mile. I wish she'd give up that behavior. I wish she'd understand that her leash releases her from being lost or hit by a car or mauled by a larger dog. I wish she'd relax and accept the inevitable. Then she could enjoy that first half mile. After all, it's just as filled with dog-thrilling sights, sounds, and smells as the rest of the walk. Unfortunately, Clare will never know that.

Accepting her leash could set Clare free.

It works for people too. We may feel like yanking and gnashing at our financial, occupational, and family obligations. We may believe we are freeing ourselves by indulging in too much food, drink, yelling, or yearning. But what must be, must be. As many a member of a religious order has discovered, if we accept our constrained circumstances, if we relax and enjoy our walk together, we may well have greater freedom. Freedom to explore our deepest selves. Freedom to listen to God. Freedom to dream up acts of community and kindness. A little more internal leashing would likely release us rather than hold us back.

It's something to think about as we prepare the altar and ourselves for Lent.

—————— What's Right with You ——————

Then Jesus said to [Bartimaeus], "What do you want me to do for you?" The blind man said to him, "My teacher, let me see again." Jesus said to him, "Go; your faith has made you well." Immediately he regained his sight and followed him on the way.
—Mark 10:51–52

One Sunday morning during the ten o'clock service, I was sitting in a pew next to the Altar Guild member on duty when the celebrating priest hesitated, searched around, then opened the rail and left the chancel. Soon she returned with a folded white cloth in her hand.

The member beside me slid down in the pew, laid her face in her hands and moaned. "Oh, no," she whispered. "I forgot the corporal! It's right there on the checklist! I must be as blind as that man in the Gospel!"

"Hey," I whispered back. "We all forget things."

As she shook her head, I thought about how we focus more on our mistakes than on our successes. Unfortunately, it's a human tendency. Then I recalled a cartoon drawn by P. Reilly for the *New Yorker* some years back. A man in his underwear sits on the examining table as a doctor reads his X-ray.

The doctor says, "Basically, there's nothing wrong with you that what's right with you can't cure."

Jesus tried to tell us that very thing.

Take Bartimaeus. For Jesus, his infirmity wasn't important. Yes, Bartimaeus was blind. But look what he had going for him! Courage and a good strong voice, to start with. Most of all, he possessed unshakable faith in a Messiah he couldn't even see. Instead of someone who was blind, Jesus saw a whole and worthy person. What was right with Bartimaeus more than made up for what was wrong.

I leaned again toward my friend as the priest began consecrating the elements. "Look at all the things up there!" I whispered, pointing at each one. "Exactly as they should be. Look at all the things you didn't forget!"

Finally she smiled, nodded, and relaxed.

It helps to remember, when we feel burdened by our flaws and mistakes, that God's checklist of what is right with each of us is longer than we can know.

ॐ

───── A Clean White Cloth ─────

The Holy Table is spread with a clean white cloth during the
celebration.

—*Book of Common Prayer, 406;*
Book of Alternative Services (Canada), 183

"A clean white cloth." What a simple rubric!

The beauty of the altar, with its gleaming white cloths, helps draw us to the contemplation and worship of God.

In our parish we call the main altar covering *fair linen,* but it is actually made of a blend of fabrics that are partly synthetic. We still have true fair linen in the sacristy cupboard, but we seldom use it. Not only that, we don't wash or iron our fair linen by hand because it's so big and unwieldy. We send it out to be professionally cleaned and pressed.

Of course linen is quite wonderful, and traditional. It was made from flax in the fields of the Holy Land in biblical times, in much the same way as it is today, and "fine linen" is mentioned several times in the Bible. I truly admire those Altar Guilds who still maintain the linen tradition and who hand-care for every single cloth used at the Eucharist. A special satisfaction must come from that.

But whether linen in name or linen in fact, fair linen is a tablecloth pure and simple. It's there to come between the precious elements and whatever surface lies beneath.

That surface is not always a formal altar.

The "clean white cloth" could be an institutional towel spread for an improvised Eucharist on the hospital bedside table of a young woman gaunt and gray with cancer. It could be a laundered shirt, jerked from a drawer as the floodwaters rise, and later spread reverently on the concrete windowsill of a homeless shelter. It could be a hand-washed terry cloth towel spread over hot sand on a remote island beach where a scientific expedition has come to study the effects of global warming on an animal species. It could be a cherished pillowcase, embroidered by a great-grandmother, dug from a worn suitcase by an immigrant seeking freedom and spread on any available surface in a ship's crowded steerage. Or it could be a cotton handkerchief from the pocket of a chaplain in khaki, weighted with stones on a windy hillock beside a mortally wounded soldier.

Rough cotton or fine linen, God doesn't care. What matters is our need for God's presence wherever we may be.

May it be that sometimes, as I work over the smooth white altar cloths in my serene church building, I will think of these other places, other circumstances, other of God's children, and send up a prayer for them.

ॐ

Box Elder Bugs

All things bright and beautiful,
all creatures great and small,
all things wise and wonderful,
the Lord God made them all.

—Hymnal, #405; CP, #415, #416

Including box elder bugs.

Our dry northern part of the country hosts relatively few insects. The creature most likely to show up at Eucharist uninvited is the box elder bug, a beetle named for a tree. It's black and orange, has wings, and is about the size of a watermelon seed.

Our Altar Guild has a small silver plate and spoon intended to remove wafer crumbs from the chalice. But we seldom set it out except in fall, which is box elder bug season. Upon finding a bug in the wine, one is to dip it out with the spoon and lay it (gasping for breath?) on the plate.

New members to whom this is explained tend to wince or shudder satisfactorily. Actually it's never happened, so far as I know, in my time at the church. But we're ready if it ever does. The possible reaction of a worshiper about to drink from a chalice containing a swimming box elder bug doesn't bear too much thinking about. Not if one wishes to stay sober-minded in the sanctuary.

Prevention is best, so we are supposed to remove the critters from the area whenever we see them. Some members can kill them easily. I can't. When I see a bug on the fair linen, I think of my mother's way of dealing with insects in her house. She would kill mosquitoes and ants, but she would rather shoo or carry flies, moths, and beetles out the door to freedom.

I am my mother's daughter. If, as I work, I see a box elder bug making her slow and trackless way across the great expanse of white, I sometimes let her continue on her chosen path. Wouldn't I often like people to let me continue on mine? Other times I pick her up, ignoring the tickly movement of her infinitesimal legs, and put her outside. Wouldn't I sometimes like people to save me from possible destruction?

Even the creatures that are neither bright nor beautiful can teach us something. An unthinking callousness toward any of God's creation is not a trait we should encourage in ourselves or in one another.

May we, today, try consciously to cherish the small things that share our lives.

——— Where Thieves Break In ———

*Do not store up for yourselves treasures on earth, where moth and
rust consume and where thieves break in and steal; but store up
for yourselves treasures in heaven...For where your treasure is,
there your heart will be also.*

—Matthew 6:19, 21

Thieves came last night.

The sacristy window is shattered. The locked cupboard was broken into
and the chalices are gone, along with the patens and the lavabo bowl. The extra
wine is gone too.

The police were here, asking us questions. They dusted for fingerprints.
They took pictures. They told us that two kinds of thieves take religious
objects: inexperienced ones who don't realize how hard they are to sell, and
experienced ones who have a way to sell them. This looked, they said, like ama-
teur work but they couldn't be absolutely sure. They said they would do their
best. They were hopeful. Now they're gone.

The director was called, and a few seasoned members, and they've arrived.
What to do? That's easy. Borrow what we need from other churches! We call

around, and a few people leave to get the things while the rest of us wait.

We feel bereft and heavy-hearted.

"Let's hope the thieves needed the money to feed a starving family," one of us says, her voice hard with sarcasm.

"Yeah, right," someone else says.

A seasoned member says, "It's the large chalice I miss most. I know we're insured and can get another. But I was used to that one."

"Those things were ours!" a young member cries. "If they can steal them, what can't they steal?"

Someone opens a Bible and reads from Matthew.

I say, "What does that mean, do you think, to lay up treasures in heaven?"

"I think," a new member says tentatively, "it means if you're the best person you can be now, you have a head start on being the right kind of person for heaven."

We look at her and smile, quickly coming to know her and to be glad she's there. She hasn't said much until now. But what she has just said is precious.

Soon someone says, "Tell you what. Let's try to pray for the thieves."

And that is what we do. We bend our heads and privately talk to God. In my prayer I recall my own experiences with having done wrong, with desiring what I should not have, with feeling unloved and hopelessly needful. After a few moments someone prays aloud, asking God to bless the people who did this thing. Almost as an afterthought, someone prays for the return of our silver.

When the borrowed things come, we set up the altar. Soon we leave the church with hearts that are almost light. Will we get our things back? We don't know. But it's all right.

They're only earthly treasures, after all.

෯

One Chalice

*During the Great Thanksgiving, it is appropriate that there be
only one chalice on the Altar, and, if need be, a flagon of wine
from which additional chalices may be filled after the Breaking of
the Bread.*

—Book of Common Prayer, 407

On my breakfront shelf is a one-handled pottery container about eight inches tall, painted black on red with a peaceful design of female figures and horses. From my late father's antiquities collection, it is a Greek oil jar dating back to 500 B.C.

Can you imagine? Five hundred years before Christ, and not very far from where this jar sat in some other woman's house, the Jews were building the Second Temple. My mind whirls just thinking about it.

I sometimes hold the jar and run my finger over the cool, smooth surface. It's not so different from the other containers in my household. It is very like the glass pitcher my New York roommate gave us as a wedding gift and the oil and vinegar set I bought last year at the local supermarket.

I think of the woman who held it long ago, a woman who, like you and me, was made in God's image. We may have had much in common, that other woman and I. She may have used the jar as she worried about her children, her husband, her pains. Other times she may have carried it lightly as she sang with joy and gratitude for the glorious dawn, or the sweet-smelling evening, the love in her heart, and the abundance of the oil.

With that single, unique jar as a catalyst, I feel a commonality with that Grecian woman transcending space and time. I know God's care is great enough to encompass us not only the two of us but more, much more, than I can possibly imagine.

So it is with the single, unique chalice I'm privileged to place on the altar on Sunday morning. Holding it, I feel a commonality with all the people who have handled and drunk from it over the years and who will handle and drink from it after I am gone.

May the singularity of the chalice symbolize for us the Oneness of God and the unity of God's people in Christ Jesus.

———————— Bread for Our Journey ————————

He told them another parable: "The kingdom of heaven is like yeast that a woman took and mixed in with three measures of flour until all of it was leavened."

—*Matthew 13:33*

Traditionally we use unleavened bread, wafers, at the Eucharist because the Last Supper was a Passover meal, taken in memory of the Israelites' hasty Exodus from Egypt. But in the Episcopal Church, we may use leavened bread for the Eucharist if we so choose. In some parishes, members responsible for setting up the altar each week also bake the Communion bread.

The other day I made bread, the leavened kind, not for Communion but for my family and friends. Bread making isn't easy. A person must want to do it and must know how. That's not all. The baker also needs strength, trust, and warmth.

It struck me as I worked that bringing about God's Rule on earth requires just about the same things.

To make bread, we follow a recipe. Certain ingredients must be used, certain procedures followed. If we ignore the wisdom passed down to us by previous breadmakers and do our own thing, our loaf will probably turn out badly.

We need physical strength as we add flour to the dough and knead it for ten or fifteen minutes. Then, when we set the bowl under a damp towel and wait, we must trust that the dough will rise when we aren't looking. Much warmth is needed too: warm water, warm air, and an even warmer oven.

Like bread baking, Kingdom-bringing takes intent, know-how, strength, trust, and warmth.

We must want to follow the rules for living that Jesus laid out for us, rules that add up to caring for one another as for ourselves. If we follow our own selfish, thoughtless ways, our lives will probably turn out badly. We need strength to work hard, as we help one another along on our journeys. We need trust because God's Rule seems to come about ever so slowly, when we aren't looking. We need warmth, because without warmth in our hearts nothing we do matters very much.

We humans require bread in order to live, bread both actual and spiritual. All bread nourishes both body and soul, but Communion bread does so in a special way.

Next time I prepare the altar for Communion, I'll think about how bread is made, how the Kingdom is brought about, and how nothing worth having comes easy.

ॐ

Wedding Details

Give them wisdom and devotion in the ordering of their common life, that each may be to the other a strength in need, a counselor in perplexity, a comfort in sorrow, and a companion in joy. Amen.
—*Book of Common Prayer, Marriage, 429;*
Book of Alternative Services (Canada), 534

"The ceremony's tomorrow, and the bride wants *what?*"

It could be almost anything. Open candle flames along the aisle. Banks of flowers obscuring the altar. Songs with questionable lyrics. Intrusive video cameras.

"Whose house is it anyway?" we members fume. We are so used to focusing on God's altar that we are upset by some wedding couples who seem not even to see it.

But behind our irritation is compassion and concern for the young couple. We know something of what lies ahead for them. We know how much they will need God. If only they could know what we know! So we recite the rules for being married in our church, but what we'd really like to say is: "You're in God's house for the most important ceremony of your life! Please, please, don't get lost in the details! Don't fuss because your maid of honor's dress clashes with the carpet!

Rejoice in her presence beside you. Don't wrangle with your parents about where they should sit! Soon you and they will be far apart. Look around! Signs of God's nearness are everywhere. Listen carefully! The words of the ceremony are wise."

What we'd like to say is that wedding details don't matter in the long run. It's the marriage details that make all the difference. The small daily courtesies. The heart-meant forgiveness and acceptance of forgiveness. The bright moments of laughter. The coming together in times of searing pain, in times of soaring joy. The day-to-day accumulation of memories.

It isn't up to us members whether or not the couple marrying in our church tomorrow will draw from the setting and from the ceremony all there is to draw. With God's grace, they will. With God's grace, they will look around, will listen, and will remember when they need to remember. I know I have recalled my wedding ceremony when I needed to, more than once, as perhaps you have recalled yours.

The next time we help prepare the sanctuary for a wedding, let us do what we can to uphold the tradition, dignity, beauty, and power of the service. It's all we can do, and when we've done that, we may calmly and prayerfully leave the details up to God.

༄

———————— Dark Stuff ————————

V., Create in us clean hearts, O God;
R., And sustain us with your Holy Spirit.

—Book of Common Prayer, 98;
Book of Alternative Services (Canada), 97

On a regular schedule, we polish the brass lectern, pulpit, missal stand, vases, altar cross, processional cross. Each job takes time and concentration, and I'm always surprised by the amount of dark stuff that comes off on my polishing cloth after the cleaning agent has been applied.

Where does it come from? The air outside in our small, non-industrial western city seems pure and clear. The air inside seems even more so.

Yet there the dark stuff is, plain to see. No getting around it. The objects and fixtures look much shinier after we've polished them, at least in our own eyes. We don't expect comment from the congregation, so we take a moment to stand back and admire one another's work:

"That altar cross really gleams!"

"You think so? I did my best. Nice job on the missal stand!"

"Thanks!"

It seems to me that prayer and meditation can do a similar polishing job on our hearts and souls. We may not be praying for change in the way we are. We may not think we especially need improvement that day or that much is wrong with us at the moment. But if we take time to concentrate on opening ourselves to God, if we let God speak to us, if we let God take the lead, we can almost feel the dark stuff coming off! All our petty, unkind, unworthy thoughts and feelings rub away and are gone. All our obsessive, nagging worries disappear.

Afterwards we may not look different or seem different—to anyone else. We certainly don't expect, or even want, someone to say, "My! How shiny you are this morning!"

But we know that our hearts and souls gleam brighter after our prayers than they did before. God knows it, too.

Hasn't it been a while since I took twenty minutes to pray and meditate? If I can't do it right now, when can I?

I'll schedule a time, a regular time, and keep to it.

༉

Blessed Forgetfulness

Time, like an ever-rolling stream,
bears all our years away;
they fly, forgotten, as a dream dies
at the opening day.

—Hymnal, #680; CP, #528

The way time blurs memory is a sad thing, yes, but it can be a blessing as well.

The other day, as I was working around the altar, a former parishioner, who had lived in Oregon for decades, came in. She was back, she told me, for an aunt's funeral.

She gazed around the sanctuary she had known as a child. "Oh, yes! I remember the Last Supper carving, and the stained glass windows, and the red carpet. But I forgot that the organ was there, and the altar steps, and the choir stalls." She sighed. "I really didn't remember it very well at all."

"You remembered the best parts," I said.

She smiled. "Why, yes. Yes, I'm glad for that."

One doesn't have to leave town for forty years to forget things. In our parish, we members each serve about six times a year. But many of us still find ourselves studying the "Vesting the Chalice" chart on the wall every time we come!

That sort of forgetfulness is only mildly embarrassing. Sometimes, though, the flowing waters of time can bear away cherished memories. The name of my best friend in fourth grade? I can see her so clearly, white-blonde hair in bangs, but her name escapes me. The appearance of that California sanctuary where our older son, Tom, was baptized? It's no use. Some things are swept away forever.

But rivers can also cleanse, can free us of old resentments, hurts, and guilts. What my junior high camp bunkmate said to me that made me cry all night? Hmm, can't recall, so maybe it wasn't so awful. What I did at age five that shamed me so much I hid under the front porch for two hours? Don't remember. Whatever it was, my parents forgave me when they found out.

Next time we fuss because we've forgotten where the baptismal shell is kept or who gave us our favorite vase, let us be thankful for the troubling memories that are also gone forever.

⌇

Pray Always

Then Jesus told them a parable about their need to pray always and not to lose heart.

—*Luke 18:1*

We Altar Guild members are lucky to have the sanctuary as our workplace, because prayer reminders surround us there. If as we work we are fully aware of where we are, we will pray.

In the Luke story, Jesus goes on to tell the parable of the woman who kept pleading her case until finally she received justice. We learn from it that persistent prayer can work wonders, in some ways we understand and in some ways known only to God.

One way persistent prayer works is that as we listen to ourselves we come to realize what truly matters to us. We may then be moved to take action. A new member I know found herself troubled by the plight of the hungry. Her attention was caught and held by articles and television stories about the problem. "Feed the hungry, Lord," she prayed always.

Once, as she worked and prayed in the sanctuary, she saw as if for the first time the basket we keep by the chancel steps for food donations. Her heart was moved, and after that, every time she came to work she brought a sack of groceries. She knows the problem is huge and outside her control, and so the hungry remain in her prayers. But she feels better because she is doing something for them.

Sometimes, when we pray always, as for recovery from a chronic illness for ourselves or someone else, nothing seems to be happening. Then our persistent prayer acknowledges that we don't always know best. God does. God has The Plan; we don't. We keep praying then because we need the strength to endure and to accept whatever happens. We pray not that God's will may be bent to ours, but ours to God's.

If we pray always, we will find ourselves asking for a parking spot when we're late for our child's concert, or for the willpower to lose five pounds before an important reunion. Should we bother God with such things? I believe so. I believe that we need to be authentic with God, to show God our whole selves. Do we really think God will be angry or disillusioned with us for small prayers? God, who knows our desires before we do? No, of course not! When we give over to God all that is in our hearts, we show our complete trust. We accept the great gift of God's unconditional love.

Let me remember, as I pray today in God's house or away from it, that the only prayer displeasing to God is the prayer that remains unprayed.

კ

──────── Stripping the Altar ────────

On this day the ministers enter in silence.
—Book of Common Prayer, 276;
Book of Alternative Services (Canada), 308

In silence and in sorrow. What is there to say? Everything is gone. We took it away ourselves, the night before, to symbolize the disciples' bereavement as Jesus is hanged on the cross.

In our church, we strip the altar and chancel area on Maundy Thursday. Chalice. Purificator. Paten. Corporal. Cruets. Breadbox. Lavabo bowl. Towel. Torches. Missal stand. Flower vases. Alms basins. Candlesticks. Reserve sacrament. Oil stock. Sanctuary light. All gone, carried out by the members on duty or in the congregation, and any other parishioners who care to help.

Back in the sacristy, we try to avoid stepping on each other as we find places for the objects we carry. Our worried expressions are very real indeed. With the cloths and the vessels gone, with the chancel empty, we are bereft and empty, too. Our hands feel heavy and useless at our sides. Jesus has left us, so what is there now for our hands to do?

My father died eleven years ago, in October. The next Good Friday, as I

Meditations for Altar Guild Members – 71

gazed at the empty chancel, my mind flashed back to the way Father's bedroom looked after he was taken to the hospital for the last time. All his life he'd written articles; each of his days, since I came to know him, contained a manuscript in progress. But that day the books were shelved, the typewriter covered, the marked-up manuscripts shut away. His clothes were hung out of sight in a closet. His bed was flat and neat. He was gone, gone from the house forever. Grief flooded me, threatened to sweep me from my feet.

Now, standing at the chancel door, I was as rocked by anguish as I had been on that other dark day. A friend saw my face and laid her hand on my shoulder. The gesture brought me to tears, but it comforted me, too.

Sermons at the Good Friday service often ask us to imagine ourselves back in time two thousand years, to imagine those dark days before the Resurrection when death meant death and Jesus was gone from the house forever. We can't really do it. Resurrection knowledge, taught to us at mother's knee, is heart-knowledge even before that. But if anything can bring us close to understanding the state of mind of those first disciples, it is the stark drama of the altar stripping.

May we draw close and comfort one another as we struggle through our personal and communal Good Fridays. May a memory of this terrible day, of all our terrible days, serve to heighten the joy that we know will soon follow.

꒰

Serving with Mirth

All people that on earth do dwell, sing to the Lord with cheerful voice; him serve with mirth, his praise forth tell, come ye before him and rejoice.

—Hymnal, #377; CP, #349

The young member-in-training had brought her visiting grandmother. The older woman leaned heavily on a cane and her granddaughter's arm as together they entered the chancel where we were working. Holy Week was approaching, so the crew was larger than usual.

"Gran used to be on the Altar Guild here," the member-in-training said. "She asked to come with me today."

We greeted her warmly. Her name was familiar, though none of us had been in the parish long enough to have worked with her.

"I'll just sit in the choir here and watch," the older woman said. Then she sighed. "I'd be on an Altar Guild still, if I could. But these days I'm too unsteady on my pins and my sight isn't what it was…"

Her voice trailed.

A lump came to my throat. As I hurried back and forth, up and down the few steps to the altar, I became especially aware of, and thankful for, my vision and the strength in my legs. The others may have been thinking along those lines, too, because we didn't talk much.

After a while, the retired member said, "Some of my happiest times were working with the Guild. I never took a job outside the home, and the Guild was the closest I ever had to a work group. How we would laugh some days! I think we quite scandalized a few of those old Fathers."

"Well, that hasn't changed," I said.

"No," someone else said. "Remember when we knocked the Bible off the lectern last month, what that supply priest muttered? I didn't think clergy knew such words!"

We laughed, the retired member along with us.

"Oh my, I can just imagine," she said, and her clouded blue eyes seemed to sparkle. "When you girls are finished, I'll tell you about the time we mislaid the wafer supply on Easter morning. Oh, and the time we were using opaque pewter cruets and switched the wine and water by mistake." She grinned. "Then there was the morning the acolyte was swinging his feet back and forth under his bench and kicked out a dead mouse!"

Instantly we decided we were as finished as we needed to be. We gathered around her with our cleaning rags in our hands. What stories we told that day! How we laughed!

Let's not get so task and goal oriented that we forget to be a congenial work group. Work groups in offices, in factories, and on farms get breaks and time to relax. Why not in churches? We're quite solemn enough there, most of the time. God loves our worship and our penitence, certainly, but God loves our mirth as well.

Plenty for All

For you, O Lord, are good and forgiving, abounding in steadfast love to all who call on you.

—*Psalm 86:5*

When we count out the wafers for Communion, they slip easily along our fingers into the silver container. So many! One of them will be ours alone, but there's no way of knowing which. Or which sip of wine is ours, either. Most of the bread and most of the wine will go to other people: people we love, people we feel kindly toward, people we try to avoid, people we barely know, and strangers.

Imagine for a moment what would happen if Communion bread were distributed according to the ways of the world. Then the millionaire CEO would have dozens of wafers poured into his hands while the mother on welfare would receive, at best, a crumb.

Or imagine that we had individual power to determine who gets what. I'm afraid we would start by holding back a few dozen for ourselves and our family. What's left we would distribute at the rail, and our personal feelings might well enter in. The woman who wrote the sympathetic note during our difficult time would get several wafers. But the man who made the sneering remark that got back to us? Hah! Just let him try to pull even one from our gripping fingers!

Of course these examples are ludicrous. Thanks be to God they are! They show how unique to our experience and how wonderful the Eucharistic meal is. No one will be offered more than one wafer, one sip of wine. No one will be offered less. There will be plenty for all.

The concept of "plenty for all" isn't easy. We humans have, from our infancy or from our personal history, a strong sense of scarcity. There may not be enough! What if there isn't enough? What if we are left without? We could die!

But Jesus brings us the news that, with God, there is always enough and more than enough to go around. Jesus tells us that under God's reign there are jars and jars of wine, portions of fish to spare, loaf after loaf of bread with basketsful left over. God promises an abundance of grace, an abundance of life, an abundance of the Spirit!

As I pour the Communion wafers into the Breadbox next Saturday, may their numbers inspire me to be more openhanded and generous with what I personally have to share.

ॐ

The Chinese Vases

And be kind to one another, tenderhearted, forgiving one another, as God in Christ has forgiven you.

—Ephesians 4:32

"I'm so afraid of breaking something or denting something or losing something," the new member said as we washed the Communion vessels. "I'm always doing that at home."

"What do you do then?" I asked.

"Get mad at myself. If it's something my husband or kids liked, they get mad at me too."

"But not for long."

"No. Still. These church things seem especially valuable, especially sacred."

So I told her a story. I told her that Father collected antiquities. My favorites were twin white vases made of fragile eggshell pottery, six inches tall, with red and black drawings of Chinese warriors.

In third grade we studied China, and I asked to take the vases to school. At first my parents said no. But I begged. I would be really, really careful! Anyway, the teachers were locking all the exhibits safely away in a display cabinet. So they let me.

Somehow a boy got into the cabinet, took out the vases to look at, and dropped them. Each broke into a dozen pieces. Feeling wretched, I dragged myself home, carrying the pieces in a box. The accident hadn't exactly been my fault. But I knew how much my father cherished those vases, and now they were ruined because of something I had done.

Mother was sorry, wished it hadn't happened, knew how bad I must feel. I could tell she was no more eager than I for Father to come home from work.

Together we showed him the pieces in the box. His jaw tightened and his face went white. "I said it was a bad idea!"

Mother drew him aside and they talked in low voices. When they looked at me again, they said, "These things happen." But I wasn't comforted. Something besides pottery had been shattered—my self-image as a good and trustworthy child.

That night I cried myself to sleep.

But next morning, the Chinese vases were back on the breakfront shelf! I couldn't believe my eyes! Had yesterday's disaster been a bad dream?

No. A closer look showed the dark glue lines, the small hole where a piece was lost back at the school. My parents had stayed up for hours, painstakingly gluing those vases back together! Not to restore their value. That was impossible. They did it so that I could feel good about myself again.

"I still have those vases," I said. "They aren't sacred in a technical sense, but they are to me because of what they mean. They remind me of what human forgiveness can be! So they're even more valuable than they would be intact.

"God forgives that same way," she said.

"Even better," I said. "With God, no glue lines show."

⌇

Marthas and Marys

Now as they went on their way, he entered a certain village, where a woman named Martha welcomed him into her home. She had a sister named Mary, who sat at the Lord's feet and listened to what he was saying.

—Luke 10:38–39

We members are Marthas when we set up the altar to welcome Jesus into our church home. We are Marys when we sit back down in the congregation and listen to the Word.

Each of us is both.

The first Labor Day after my retirement from the school district wasn't easy. The bell rang, the school doors opened and closed without me. No desk or message box, no district directory carried my name. No young faces looked at me expectantly. No work group laughed with me at lunch.

Was I no longer a laborer? I went to the dictionary and found that to labor is "to exert one's powers of body or mind." No mention there of producing or succeeding or earning or climbing the corporate ladder. To exert one's powers! Something we all do just by living fully. Many members hold jobs outside the home, but many others do not. Those of us who never have been or are no longer in the paid labor force still have great powers of body and mind.

After Jesus' death and Resurrection, we know what Martha did. She went right on keeping house—however sad and distracted she must have been at first. Perhaps she opened her doors to certain of the faithful who wished only to be where Jesus had been.

But what about her sister? Did Mary of Bethany lose heart, sit staring into space, or go into an early decline? I don't think so. I think she recalled what she learned at Jesus' feet. I think she labored on for love of God, self, and neighbor as long as possible. Perhaps people sat at her feet while she passed along what she had learned. Perhaps she used stitchery or gardening to impart her understanding of God's love. Perhaps she expressed her unique insights simply by the way she ordered her days, responded to friends, greeted strangers.

Like those long-ago sisters, we members offer our thoughts, hearts, and labor to God and one another. Martha or Mary, doing or hearing, let us welcome every chance we have to use our powers fully.

☙

A Beam of Light

May choirs of angels lead you to Paradise on high.

—Hymnal, #356

Before a burial service, we lay out the heavy pall, the purpose of which is to make the cheapest coffin and the most expensive equal, as we all are, before God. Our funeral pall is purple, though many churches use white to show that we gather to celebrate a life and the certainty of resurrection.

Usually we members will attend the service after preparing the sanctuary, even if we knew the deceased only slightly. We know it is a celebration, but we are sad to lose any member of our parish family.

A church building often feels closed and oppressive at a burial service. Even white vestments can look weighty and constraining on the ministers, while the somber clothing of the mourners seems to draw in the very walls. The coffin, or the urn, looks so heavy, so still, so final.

We of the gathered community listen hard to the lyrical words of the prayer book, the consoling words of the clergy, and the brave words of relatives. But wonderful as they are, not even those words can ease our burden.

Only faith can, faith and grace.

I remember the burial service of a parishioner who was not young when he died but whose good cheer had never diminished. In front of me sat a restless child of four or five, a great-grandchild of the deceased. He wore a miniature dark blue suit that bunched up as he squirmed, and throughout the service he bounced back and forth from the pew to his mother's lap. But he didn't whine or complain; he was as quiet as he could be, and his mother often bent to whisper praise and counsel patience.

Toward the end of the service, a beam of light slipped through a yellow panel of a stained glass window and touched the coffin, causing that section of pall to shine like amethyst.

As I watched, the little boy reached out a finger, held it close to his face, and traced the path of that beam. A simple thing, but the way he did it took my breath away. His small finger moved smoothly along the light, not from window to coffin but the other way. It moved from coffin to window...and beyond!

The child may not have heard a word that was said that day, but intuitively he seemed to understand, probably better than most of the rest of us did, the spirit of the gathering.

Let us recall, as we prepare the church and ourselves for a burial service, that death is only a release into joy and light.

࿐

Easter People

Jesus Christ is risen today, Alleluia!
our triumphant holy day, Alleluia!
who did once upon the cross, Alleluia!
suffer to redeem our loss, Alleluia!

—*Hymnal, #207; CP, #203*

The Easter Vigil begins in darkness, then the Paschal Candle is lit, then the altar candles. By Easter Morning, we have set out each candelabra and turned every switch, so that all the lights in the sanctuary flicker, flame, and shine.

With the light there are the flowers, those creamy, fragrant ranks of lilies that are bought by parishioners in memory of loved ones and set out in special holders.

The lavish setting we members prepare opens us to the extravagant, miraculous promise of Easter.

One of my favorite seasonal readings is the one from the Prophet Ezekiel in which dry bones are miraculously reconnected and refleshed to breathe and move again. We can respond to it because of the promise of eternal life, and also because we are, in this earthly life, Easter people. We all experience small resurrections, all the time. Every spring. Every morning. Day to day, we are brought from despair to renewed hope, from weariness to bursts of energy, from doubt to strong faith. By the grace of God, when we are the most dispirited, when we feel most disconnected and dry, our hearts suddenly change and our spirits soar.

Easter moments happen to all of us, but they are easiest to recognize when they happen dramatically: when a handicapped child of eight learns to ask for what he needs; when a middle-aged woman enters her kitchen to cook supper for the first time after her near-fatal heart attack; when a young woman ready to take a hit of heroin unties the band from her arm, flees that awful place, and gets on a bus to return to her parents; when a young man caught in terrible circumstances finishes his sentence and walks from the jail into the sweet fresh air, into the arms of his wife and children.

Alleluia! Alleluia!

As we decorate the church for this greatest of Christian celebrations, let's thank God for our own Easter moments from the year past. Then let's remember Jesus' Resurrection, and sing our favorite hymn aloud for the wonder of it!

ॐ

Legacy

Their bodies are buried in peace,
*   but their name lives on generation after generation.*
The assembly declares their wisdom,
*   and the congregation proclaims their praise.*

—Sirach 44:14–15

Several of us members were polishing things in the sacristy, getting ready for the new church year, when a member-in-training who was working on the missal stand ran her finger over the name engraved on the base.

"Does anyone know who this is?" she asked, reading it out.

No one did.

"I think that's sad," she said. "I mean, how we're forgotten even when our name is on something."

Nobody said anything for a while. Then a seasoned member said, "That's so. But people close to us remember us, and more by the small things we do and say than by any big, famous thing. At a picnic last summer, my youngest cousin quoted something I was supposed to have said years ago. Told me she'd always taken guidance from it. My goodness, I didn't remember saying any such thing!"

We laughed.

"But it was something you agreed with?" I said.

"Well, yes. It rang true to me."

"Then maybe even though you didn't actually say it, you've lived your own life that way."

"Could be."

"It's not up to us, how we're remembered," a new member said. "Take our children. Half the time they want to be just like us. Half the time they want to be the exact opposite!"

We laughed again. "Got that right."

After a while, the seasoned member said, "My best girlfriend lost her baby brother years ago. He was too young to pass along very much. But I've come to think he lives on by the way he changed and affected her, and she in turn affected me, and so on." She smiled. "To me it's like ripples in water, touching other ripples."

"It is, isn't it?" I said. "Very like that. On and on, through time and through space, in ways we can't even imagine."

"So what do we do to be remembered in good ways?" the new member asked.

The seasoned member thought a moment, and then she said, "As you say, it's not really up to us. But I guess we try to do the best we can, with God's help."

We all nodded, agreeing. The member-in-training sighed. "Okay. But I'd really like for us to pray for this person," and she pointed again to the name in the brass.

So that was what we did.

Dear God, we thank you for those who have gone before, in our lives and in our work. Help us to conduct our own lives and work so that the way we touch others may always be to your honor and glory. Amen.

౨

———— Prayers for Altar Guilds ————

On entering for work

Dear God, be with us this day as we prepare the sanctuary for your people. Make us humble as your instruments, skilled as your creation, reverent in your service. Help us not to let the form of things blind us to their sacred purpose, or personal concerns deafen us to the needs of others. In Jesus' name we pray. Amen.

On leaving for home

Dear God, we have completed the tasks set for us today. Thank you for allowing us this service. May we carry back into the world and into our homes some of the holy mystery that has surrounded us here, through Jesus Christ our Lord. Amen.

On preparing to worship

Dear God, before us lies the altar we have helped to prepare. We now freely offer it to you and to the community gathered in your honor, as we turn and ready ourselves to worship you. This we do for Jesus' sake. Amen.